Follow the Flyway

The Marvel of Bird Migration

words by
Sarah Nelson

art by
Maya Hanisch

Barefoot Books
step inside a story

Across the cool, green north in springtime,
nests are crafted, cushioned, hidden
among the trees, between the reeds
in marshes, bogs, and sandy beaches.

Then mamas lay
    their pretty eggs
and nestle softly on them.

Days pass
and soon weeks
until...

tick, tick, tick!

tap, tap, tap!

crack! crack! crack! crack!

Lots and lots of little babies hatch.

Bald ones, fuzzy ones,
plump and round
and long and leggy ones.

They squabble
and waddle
and paddle
and gobble.

They learn to quack
or hoot or honk.

Some learn to run,
others to dive.

And eventually, always...

feathers fill in,
wings unfurl
and every baby learns to *fly!*

But autumn comes
and something changes —
even the young ones feel it.

Leaves tumble.
Weeds bow down.
The sun sets early
and rises late.

Food grows scarce,
but something else...

The wind! The sky! The south is calling!

Kwa,kwa,kwa!

Grronnk!

ta-Wheeeet!

So over the beaches, bogs, and marshes,
   out of the rushes and reeds —

      across the chilly, golden north
         in twos and tens and twenties —

   ducks, geese, and herons, giant-winged pelicans,
      egrets and sandpipers, swans, loons, and snipes

lift, lift, lift

up, up, up

into the blue and ancient flyway.

Hooup! Hooop!

Some of the young ones fly with their flocks,
    learning the route from the elders.

Some just seem to know the way

    like a map of the world is inside them.

They follow food and follow water,
the shape of the land,
the tail of the wind,

navigating with the sun and stars
and the powerful pull of the south.

On and on, they flap and sail —
below the clouds or miles high
in twos and tens and twenties and *hundreds* —

together again, chasing the river.

Splish!

Sploosh!

They feast on weeds,
dabble and bathe,
catch minnows and mussels,
and snooze in the shade.

They stay a day,
a week or so.
(The young ones
never want to go!)

But always, always...
a cold gust catches them,
mamas honk, and flocks insist.

Honk!

So up and up and on and on!
Along this highway etched in time.
Ducks, geese, and dunlins, herons and pelicans,
egrets and sandpipers, swans, loons, and snipes.

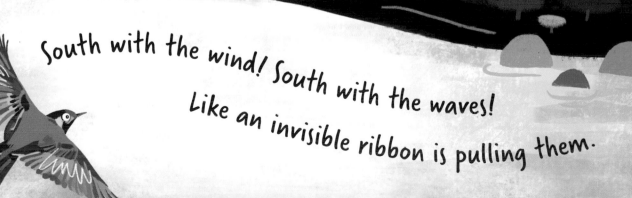

South with the wind! South with the waves!
Like an invisible ribbon is pulling them.

The young ones learn a lot of lessons
about buildings... buses...

blizzards . . . foxes . . .

grandmas . . . gardens . . .

boats . . . and barges.

They travel on. They swirl and glide.
They ride on thermals — wings spread wide.

Until, finally,
at last, at last...

the ocean.

The birds spread out across the coast —
families, flocks, and young ones all grown.

They fill the
beaches, bogs,
and bayous...
until they feel the pull of
springtime.

Fascinating Flyway Facts

What is migration?

Around the world, many birds journey from one region to another, following the seasons. These journeys are called **migration**. In North America, birds typically fly south for the winter to the southern United States, Mexico, the Caribbean or even all the way to Central and South America. In springtime, the birds return north, often to the places they were born. The long migration routes that birds follow are called **flyways** — kind of like bird highways / motorways in the sky. Birds follow these same flyways year after year, traveling the same paths and places that their great-great-grandparents did.

Why travel together?

Many birds migrate with their families or in groups called **flocks**. Adult leaders who have made the trip before show the younger birds the route and the best places to stop to rest along the way. The young birds follow and learn to spot important landmarks, such as mountains, shorelines, rivers or even large buildings. In this way, birds rely on memory, as well as their excellent senses of sight, hearing and smell to navigate the long journey.

How else do birds find their way?

Many **migratory** birds (birds that migrate) are born with an instinct for where to travel. The places they are meant to fly seem to be programmed into their brains and bodies. Birds' amazing sense of direction helps them get there. In fact, birds can actually feel the earth's magnetic pulls. Like a compass, a bird feels the pull of the North and South Poles and knows precisely which direction it should go. Migratory birds also use the sun and stars to find their way.

Can you watch birds migrate?

If you're lucky, you might hear migratory birds calling and look up to see them in flight. But more often, they are flying much too high for us to see. Some flap endlessly on; some flutter and then glide; some ride the wind with their wings open wide. Many birds make stops along the flyway to rest and feed, so you might spot them napping in the reeds or fishing in a lake. However, some small birds can make their whole journey without stopping.

How can we help migratory birds?

Migratory birds need us to protect their **habitats** — the places where they live and visit. This includes their breeding grounds in the north where they lay and hatch their eggs, their wintering grounds in the south where they fly to find food during colder months and all the places where they rest and feed along the way. We can help migratory birds by keeping our waterways, wetlands, parks and coastlines clean and wild, protected from pollution and human development.

The Four North American Flyways

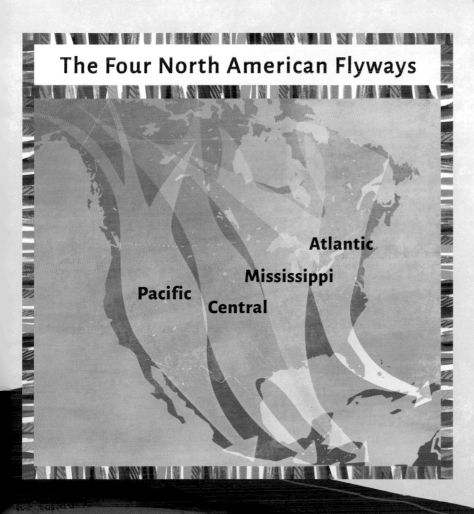

Atlantic

Mississippi

Pacific

Central

Where are the flyways?

North America has four major flyways. The settings in this book are inspired by the **Mississippi Flyway**, which is the migration path for almost half of North America's ducks and geese, as well as many other water-loving birds. The Mississippi River and the wetlands and woodlands near it provide everything these birds need — fresh water, fish, plant-filled meadows, marshes and shores, trees for roosting and hidden spots for sleeping.

Birds of the Flyway

Trumpeter Swan mothers lay one egg every other day, but they don't sit on them to warm them until they have laid a whole group of eggs (called a **clutch**). This way, all the babies hatch on the same day — one month later. Trumpeter Swans are big, heavy birds and need a large area of water for their splashy takeoffs.

Mallard ducklings can swim, waddle and find their own food within 24 hours of hatching but can't fly for two months. They have to grow their flying feathers first! Mallard flocks fly in a V shape when they migrate. If the wind is pushing them, they can travel over 600 miles (1,000 km) in one day.

Wood Ducks nest in holes in trees. When the ducklings are one day old, they leap out of their nest, fall to the ground and follow their mothers to water. Amazingly, the ducklings are so tiny and light that they don't get hurt. Unlike most ducks, wood ducks can fly through forests, swerving easily between the trees.

Canada Geese line their nests with **down**, or soft, wispy feathers that the mothers pull from their own bodies. Baby geese, called **goslings**, are always with their parents — unless a few families take turns babysitting. Canada Geese migrate in large flocks and do a lot of noisy honking as they fly.

Common Loons sometimes swim with their babies on their backs to protect them from hungry **predators** (animals that might try to eat them) like snapping turtles. Loons catch fish while swimming very fast underwater. They can also fly up to 75 miles (120 km) per hour. That's as fast as a cheetah running at top speed!

Great Blue Herons raise their babies in giant bowl-shaped nests of sticks at the tops of trees. Young herons walk about on branches, jumping and pumping their wings to get ready for their first flight. Though they often nest in large groups, Great Blue Herons migrate all alone.

Green Herons work together to build nests, warm eggs and feed their babies. These crafty birds sometimes dangle a feather or a bug in shallow water and wait for curious fish to swim over. Then *snap!* — they capture their meals. Green Herons migrate at night in flocks.

Great Egrets nest high in the trees like Great Blue Herons. Parents feed their hungry chicks by swallowing frogs, fish or other food and then spitting those meals back up. Great Egrets fly with slow, elegant wingbeats, and can travel as far south as Panama.

American White Pelicans are born bald and helpless. Eventually, pelicans have wings that span 9 ft (almost 3 m). They sail together along the flyway, swirling up, up, up on pockets of warm air called **thermals**. Then they stretch out their wings and soar.

Spotted Sandpipers teeter and bob out of the nest shortly after hatching. They learn to fly just three weeks later. Sandpipers are named for running across sandy beaches, whistling high "piping" notes like a flute: *ta-Wheeet!* Spotted Sandpipers fly low over water with very fast wingbeats, followed by brief glides.

Wilson's Snipes use their beaks to weave nests of grass. If a predator gets close to the eggs or chicks, a parent snipe will lure it away, pretending to be injured. Wilson's Snipes can zip, zigzag, and fly 60 miles (around 100 km) per hour. They migrate at night.

Dunlin chicks are tiny, fluffy and busy as soon as they are born, poking in the soil for insects. Along the flyway, Dunlins may swarm together by the thousands and fly in unison over shores. These enormous flying flocks look like waving, whirling dances.

Select Sources

Books

Elphick, Jonathan, ed. *Atlas of Bird Migration: Tracing the Great Journeys of the World's Birds.* Buffalo, New York: Firefly Books LTD, 2007.

Schneck, Marcus. *Ducks and Waterfowl: A Portrait of the Animal World.* New York, New York: Todri Productions LTD, 1999.

Websites

The Cornell Lab of Ornithology. "All About Birds: Bird Guide." Cornell University. https://www.allaboutbirds.org/guide/search/

The Cornell Lab of Ornithology. "Birds of North America." Cornell University. https://birdsna.org/Species-Account/bna/home

Kaufman, Kenn. "Guide to North American Birds." The National Audubon Society. http://www.audubon.org/bird-guide

For Further Reading

Hickman, Pamela. *Birds.* Kids Can Press, 2020. An accessible look at all things bird—life cycles, habitats, seasonal changes and more.

Markle, Sandra. *The Long, Long Journey: The Godwit's Amazing Migration.* Millbrook Press, 2013. A journey with godwits from egg-hood in Alaska to winter on New Zealand shores.

Wolfson, Elissa, and Margaret A. Barker. *Audubon Birding Adventures for Kids: Activities and Ideas for Watching, Feeding, and Housing Our Feathered Friends.* Quarry Books, 2020. A family-friendly field guide to common North American birds with engaging activities.

Zommer, Yuval. *Big Book of Birds.* W. W. Norton & Company, 2019. Answers to playful questions about eggs, feathers, beaks and birdsong with fun facts about many specific species.

For my husband, Vince, who follows the flyway birds with me — S. N.

To my family, Euge, Cleme, Domi and Toto, for being my inspiration every day — M. H.

Barefoot Books would like to thank the following people for their help in the creation of this book:
Nick Lund, Maine Audubon | Emily Golightly, Media Coordinator / Librarian, Newport Elementary School

Barefoot Books, 23 Bradford Street, 2nd Floor, Concord, MA 01742
Barefoot Books, 29/30 Fitzroy Square, London, W1T 6LQ

Text copyright © 2023 by Sarah Nelson
Illustrations copyright © 2023 by Maya Hanisch
The moral rights of Sarah Nelson and Maya Hanisch have been asserted

First published in the United States of America by Barefoot Books, Inc and in Great Britain by Barefoot Books, Ltd in 2023
All rights reserved

Graphic design by Sarah Soldano, Barefoot Books
Design assistance by Lindsey Leigh, Barefoot Books
Edited and art directed by Lisa Rosinsky, Barefoot Books
Reproduction by Bright Arts, Hong Kong. Printed in China

This book was typeset in Alegreya Sans, Bad Script, Verveine and Modish
The illustrations were created using pencils, water-based paints and digital techniques

Hardback ISBN 978-1-64686-632-8 | Paperback ISBN 978-1-64686-633-5
E-book ISBN 979-8-88859-021-8

British Cataloguing-in-Publication Data: a catalogue record for this book is available from the British Library

Library of Congress Cataloging-in-Publication Data is available under LCCN 2023930576

1 3 5 7 9 8 6 4 2